# HOW TO MANIFEST SUCCESS

# HOW TO MANIFEST SUCCESS

## 50 LESSONS IN LIFE LEADERSHIP AND LOVE

## HILTON MISSO

WILEY

First published 2026 by John Wiley & Sons Australia, Ltd

ISBN: 978-1-394-37130-3

A catalogue record for this book is available from the National Library of Australia

*Registered Office*
John Wiley & Sons Australia, Ltd. Level 4, 600 Bourke Street, Melbourne, VIC 3000, Australia

For details of our global editorial offices, customer services, and more information about Wiley products visit us at www.wiley.com.

Wiley also publishes its books in a variety of electronic formats and by print-on-demand. Some content that appears in standard print versions of this book may not be available in other formats.

Cover design by Wiley

Figure 1: © JeromeCronenberger/Adobe Stock

Set in 11/15pts and Palatino LT Std by Straive, Chennai, India.

# Contents

# Introduction

I am a simple, ordinary guy. I do not have any special talents, abilities or gifts. I am neither extraordinary nor unique. I'm just your average man. I do not say that with false modesty. It is simply the truth. But what I have done is make the most of what I have been given and in doing so, I've achieved remarkable success in all areas of my life. Now, I want to share how I did it, so you can take your own talents, as limited or as expansive as they may be, and use them to create something extraordinary, unlock your full potential and achieve the success you deserve.

I've spent 60 years in the trenches of business, first as a lawyer and then as a property developer, childcare centre operator, tech entrepreneur and in my later years, a philanthropist. Throughout my career, I've worked under the radar with the intent to be invisible, irrelevant and redundant and I've found that strategy has been absolutely effective in achieving success. Now, at 80 years of age, I believe I've earned my stripes and the right to reflect on those years and share what I've learned. My journey has given me a unique perspective on success—not just in business, but in every facet of my existence. It's taken me decades to formulate my message and it's one I am now indeed ready to share.

My life has been hard. I've had low esteem, low confidence, low everything and was 'blessed' with a weak constitution, which meant I was constantly unwell. I had a delicate build that made me look frail and inconsequential. People treated me with disdain and assumed I was unable to achieve anything. This treatment escalated during my teenage years, a period that was torturous for me, as I know it is for many. I longed to be strong, good-looking and confident—everything I wasn't.

This curse turned into a blessing when I woke up to the fact that it was not about the cards I had been dealt: it was about *how* I played the cards I'd been dealt. I was a hugely introverted young man and due to the hardships I experienced, I rarely spoke. This didn't mean I didn't think. I was always thinking, but I didn't have the confidence to express my thoughts. That silence in my mind gave me the space to listen carefully to not only what was going on *around* me, but to what was going on *within* me. The important message the silence helped me discover was that if I wanted to succeed in life (and I *desperately* wanted to succeed in life) I would need to accept the cards I was given and use them to work smarter, not harder. It helped me form the mantra I have carried through my life and is really the underlying theme of the book—that you could manifest anything that you want in life by thinking to be, anything you want to be. This became 'Think2Be—Anything You Want2Be'.

The question that then consistently presented itself to me was: If I needed to work smarter, not harder, then how could I think and *be* smarter? Working harder physically was not an option. My ill-health wouldn't permit it. So, I had to work smarter. I could figure it out through trial and error, but I was in a hurry. I had already wasted so much of my life lying in a bed with all manner of ailments. I wanted to get smarter *now*. I had to think logically about this. The crucial first step was to study the very nature of success itself. What is success? Who has it? What are the fundamental differences between the 'haves' and the 'have-nots'? If I could pinpoint the core distinctions between those two identities, I could reverse-engineer the secrets and apply them to my own life. I was definitely in the camp of the 'have-nots' so I was desperate to learn how I could make the leap into the world of the 'haves'.

# A system for success

Some people study financial markets, footy statistics or fashion. I made it my business to study success in all its facets and then use that knowledge to manifest my dreams and goals. I was introduced to the science of success when I was 16. My father, an avid student of the human condition, was aware of my hunger to improve myself and suggested I join a self-development group called Junior Chamber International, or JCI, a rotary-style club for young people. This organisation introduced me to the six critical areas of life that, if mastered, would lead to success: family, community, public speaking, career, spiritual growth and personal growth. This club opened the door to the world of self-help and personal development and I embraced everything they had to offer.

One of the most profound teachings came from a motivational program I was given that taught would-be Amway business owners the rules of the multi-level marketing game. To the casual observer, it was a course on how to get rich quick. I didn't believe in get-rich-quick schemes then (and I still don't) but I was very curious as to what this course covered. When I opened the materials, I was astounded. Yes, it was a training course on how to get rich, but it wasn't about getting rich *quick*. It was a masterclass on the law of attraction and how to attract not just financial wealth, but all forms of wealth—spiritual, physical, familial, societal—into your life. It was also a serious exploration of the kind of person you needed to *be* to attract those forms of wealth and a step-by-step guide on how to become that kind of person. It was exactly what I was looking for: an in-depth, timeless program for reprogramming my psyche to naturally attract the abundance I craved in all areas of my life.

I devoured the contents of this program, became completely obsessed with the topic and went in search of every self-help teacher, philosopher, speaker and authority I could find. I sought out Napoleon Hill. Dale Carnegie. Norman Vincent Peale. Earl Nightingale. Glenn W Turner. Jim Rohn. Zig Ziglar. Tony Robbins. John Kehoe. Wayne Dyer. Brian Tracy. Louise Hay. Jack Canfield.

Stephen R Covey. Rhonda Byrne—and many more—and devoured everything they wrote or produced on the topic of success.

I've since spent more than 60 years studying the elements of success and while I don't have a degree from the University of Harvard, I do have a PhD from the University of Hard Knocks. Despite the success I have since attained, I continue to learn much from this difficult school called 'life'.

I believe I have now earned the right to talk about how I have attracted abundant success through the belief that I can 'Think2Be anything I Want2Be', and I would like to share that system of success with you.

## So, who am I and why should you listen to me?

There is little in my life that I have truly wanted and not been able to manifest or achieve, except for one thing: Arnold Schwarzenegger's physique. I tried—believe me, I tried—but this is the one goal in my life that eluded me. On reflection, I am grateful for this. If I had been gifted with that idealised body from a young age, I may very well have ended up just an average person coasting through life, probably retired and deeply unsatisfied because I did nothing truly meaningful with my talents and drive.

Being ignored because I was skinny and shy turned out to be a gift. These challenges gave me a fierce determination to build a meaningful life. While other teenagers chased good times, my struggles forced me to develop grit and determination. I may have wanted Arnold Schwarzenegger's muscles, but overcoming my physical limitations taught me something more valuable: perseverance, creativity and belief in myself. Those early hardships inspired me to achieve great things.

With more years behind me than ahead of me (although I am planning to live to at least 105) I can see now that the myriad struggles I faced throughout my life weren't obstacles, but stepping stones that forced me to think differently, work smarter and dream bigger. My physical limitations became the catalyst for creating a life of significance, which in turn shaped the foundation of my success. They were not obstacles but the raw materials from which I carved a meaningful legacy, proving that challenges can be the very source of strength and purpose.

While I have made a lot of money from my endeavours in law, property, childcare and technology, making money was never my objective. It still isn't. Since I was a graduate lawyer, my life's goal has always been to 'do good for the many, with leverage, and have impact' in all of my pursuits. And that's what I have done.

You may not have heard of me, but within the business community, I'm best known for fundamentally transforming how Australian law firms operate. In 1989, my team and I introduced the concept of 'no win, no fee' to Australia, a service that enabled everyday people to access legal justice at no cost. This 'no win, no fee' legal service is now offered by almost all law firms in the country—some more ethically than others—and has enabled tens of thousands of low-income and disadvantaged Australians to seek justice for wrongdoings enacted upon them by bigger and more powerful entities—justice they would have been denied had it not been for this revolutionary concept. Ironically, considering it was a 'no win, no pay' concept, offering this service was a large part of why I was able to sell my law firm to Slater and Gordon for more than $57 million in 2010. More on that later.

(By the way, when I say 'I' introduced this concept to Australia, I say it with the greatest humility because, as we all know, nothing is ever done on one's own. Every success I have enjoyed has been the result of a monumental team effort. Having said that, for ease and cogency, I will use 'I' as the pronoun throughout the rest of this book. But please understand all my successes were based on team efforts.)

This corporate achievement is what most people know me for but please don't pay attention to me or my musings because of that one accomplishment. That is but one measure of my success. I feel uneasy listing my financial credentials as if they were the only metrics that mattered, but I know that financial abundance is a key measure that many use to evaluate a successful life. While I won't disclose my net worth, I can say with confidence that I've built a financial legacy that affords me complete freedom: freedom to live life on my terms, support the people and causes I care about and make an impact beyond business. It's not in my nature to big note myself (for reasons that will become apparent) but what I will reveal now and throughout this book are my secrets for how I manifested success in all aspects of my life and how, if you apply the same principles with consistency and discipline, you can too.

## Success leaves clues

If you're looking for real-world proof that my principles for manifesting success work, this book is for you. Across my life and career, I've applied, refined and tested the lessons I share in this book: lessons that have led to extraordinary success in law, business, property, technology and philanthropy. Here's a snapshot of what I've built using these principles:

- I founded and grew a law firm from a two-person team into a business that later sold for $57 million.

- I helped a company that developed a software product for the childcare industry realise $44 million in value in a four-year period.

- I built a multi-million+ real estate and asset portfolio.

- I founded a childcare company employing more than 400 educators, caring for thousands of children.

- I developed a global digital program worth many millions of dollars, providing on-demand, personalised mindfulness programs for children, educators and parents.

- I established a charitable foundation (Public Ancillary Fund) for mindfulness education and research to reach one million children by 2035.

- I developed a long-term strategy to build a $10 million foundation fund to sustainably support mindfulness projects.

- I planned the development of a 50-storey global hub for mindfulness and wellness in Moreton Bay, Queensland, dedicated to helping those on their journey of self-discovery unlock their highest potential.

On a personal level, I have been happily married to the love of my life for nearly 60 years and live in a beautiful home by the Pacific Ocean in Queensland. I am blessed with three successful adult children, eight wonderful grandchildren and a life filled with adventure, purpose and impact. Through my work and experiences, I've had the privilege of positively influencing tens of thousands of people and turning my journey into one of fulfilment, legacy and lasting contribution. It happened because I was able to 'Think2Be, Anything I Wanted2Be'.

# What to expect in this book

If you're ready to unlock the real secrets of success—not just in business, but in leadership, love and life—this book is your roadmap. It's designed to help you understand the law of attraction, align your energy and activate the inner power needed to manifest what you truly desire.

This isn't a book of theories or about following a rigid formula. It's about learning a repeatable system built on beliefs, disciplines and daily practices. It's a collection of 50 real-life lessons, each one drawn from the experiences, challenges and breakthroughs I've lived through across decades in business, law, property, philanthropy and personal growth. I'll walk you through the exact mindset shifts, strategies and decisions that turned my biggest visions into reality and outline for you how you can do the same. Applied consistently and with discipline, these lessons will show you how to:

- apply a simple formula to achieve any goal
- eliminate fear and turn adversity into opportunity
- access your intuition to find out what your true and undeniable purpose is
- develop the discipline and mindset needed to take action and manifest your goals
- reprogram your subconscious mind to attract success and abundance 24/7
- build a successful business, maximise its value and prepare it for sale
- handle betrayal, disappointment and loss in business, love and life with resilience
- uncover untapped markets and leverage them for profit and power
- know when to follow the crowd and when to be a contrarian
- stay true to your values and stick to your guns when the world is telling you to give up
- find your compelling 'why' to help you keep going when the odds are against you ...

... and much more.

This book is the culmination of my 80 years of experience: a guide for those who, like me, have felt held back by circumstances, doubt or fear. It's for the dreamers and the doers. It's for anyone who has ever asked, 'Why am I here? What am I truly capable of? How do I move past fear and into my full potential?'

If you're ready to unlock the magic within—a magic that already exists inside you, waiting to be tapped—I recommend you adopt my five principles of successful manifestation, which I'm about to outline for you. You'll discover how to harness your thoughts, transform your beliefs and manifest a life of abundance, purpose and joy beyond anything you've ever imagined. You'll soon discover that you don't need to be extraordinary to achieve extraordinary things.

# Five principles of successful manifestation

Manifestation isn't about magic, luck or lighting a sacred candle and hoping things work out. It's about alignment of intention and taking consistent action. If you want to build something meaningful, be it a business, a life or a legacy, you need more than just good ideas. You need belief, structure, self-discipline, emotional alignment and perspective. These five principles are the success engine behind manifestation. In this section, I'll show you how to use each one to turn your vision into something real. No fluff. No hype. Just a practical roadmap that works.

### Harness the power of belief

Napoleon Hill, the author of *Think and Grow Rich*, famously said, 'Conceive and believe and you will achieve'. I must have read that book 20 times and to be quite honest, I never fully understood it. But the key messages that came through clearly were that 1) success follows rules, 2) you must free yourself of all negative beliefs about your ability to achieve your goals and 3) you must believe in yourself. The last message is the most important. You can follow all the rules and do all the work, but without a bedrock belief that what you want *is* possible, you will fail to manifest even the most basic of your desires.

Numerous studies on twins have shown that *belief* is what sets people apart. You can have two people with the same parents, home life, high school, friends, degrees and everything else and yet one will manifest a life of abundance, while the other will not. One twin effortlessly attracts success, while the other struggles to keep it, no matter how hard they work. The difference? Their beliefs. Like a magnet, one twin naturally draws success to them, while the other unconsciously pushes it away.

To achieve any goal, you must truly believe you can make it happen. Take money, for example. I've created great wealth for myself and others throughout my life, but over the years I have discovered a very important and fundamental truth: most people struggle with money simply because of what they believe about it.

Let's use twins as an example. The one who manifests abundance truly believes at a cellular level that money is good; that the possession of it can serve humanity in many wondrous ways; that it is readily abundant and available and with the right application of tools and mindset, it can be manifested as readily as turning on a tap.

The twin who fails to generate financial abundance will most likely have negative beliefs—albeit subconscious—that money is inherently the manifestation of all that is bad in the world; that those who have it must have made it through ill-gotten ways; that their lives are complicated by the having of it and that people close to them will resent them for having it.

This twin will deny they have these beliefs, but if they were to move into a meditative state and ask themselves a series of probing questions about their beliefs, then score themselves and look at the sum total of their beliefs, the score would reflect their true reality of what money means to them. Invariably, they would find that at a subconscious level, they have a belief system about money that guarantees they will never rise above a certain, self-imposed level.

So, now they discover they've got a problem with their beliefs and the next question they ask is, 'Well, how do I fix this problem?' The great news is you can change your beliefs about money—about anything—using the 50 lessons outlined in this book. There are many other limiting beliefs that sabotage our pursuit of success (our sense of deserving love is one that escapes many) but financial abundance is one that eludes most. While money is by no means the salve to every issue, it is an energy that can be mastered—and needs to be mastered—to achieve your life's goals. Money has never been my motivator but it has been a useful yardstick to determine whether my strategies are working or not.

## Harness a proven system

Success isn't random and it isn't a final destination. It follows a structured process and it's a continuous journey of learning, adapting and evolving. Over the years, I've studied, tested and refined a framework that consistently leads to breakthroughs. I've called it The 5-Step Misso System for Success. Whether it's for work, wellness or wealth, these five steps give you a process to bring your goals to fruition. If you follow the process and master these principles, you'll get the clarity you need to build confidence, which will in turn create the energy needed to maintain momentum, which will drive the action and discipline needed to generate extraordinary results.

Why do we need a process? Because most people struggle not due to a lack of talent or ambition, but because they lack a *system*. The 5-Step Misso System for Success—visualisation, affirmation, seeding, belief and action—provides that structure. Without a clear roadmap, it's easy to get lost in self-doubt, procrastination or fear of failure. It helps you not only dream big but also take consistent, focused action to turn those dreams into reality. Here's a rundown of the five steps.

### 1. Visualisation: See your success clearly before it happens

Success starts in the mind. By meditating, silencing the noise, going inward and connecting with your deepest intuition, you'll find the stillness you need to gain clarity on your true nature, uncover your highest purpose and align with the unique talents you were born to express. When you can clearly see your goal and immerse yourself in its details, emotions and outcomes, you create a mental blueprint that guides your actions. What you visualise consistently, you move towards.

### 2. Affirmation: Words shape reality and repetition reinforces belief

Affirmations are the bridge between thought and reality. They shape your beliefs and reprogram your subconscious for success. By consistently repeating powerful, positive statements, you align your mind with confidence, clarity and possibility. The more you affirm, the more you rewire your thinking, shift limitations into strengths and transform aspirations into lived experience.

### 3. Seeding: Plant the right habits, ideas and influences

Every thought you entertain, every conversation you engage in and every habit you repeat is a seed. What you plant is what you grow. Apple seeds don't produce oranges—and the same goes for your thoughts, habits and relationships. By choosing wisely and reinforcing the right patterns, you shape your future. Your environment is your garden. Nurture it carefully and breakthroughs will come.

### 4. Belief: Believe it before you see it

Belief is the invisible engine behind visible success. Before others can see your vision, you must believe in it—fully, deeply and without doubt. Strong belief draws people, opportunities and momentum towards you. Action always follows belief. But even one hidden thread of doubt can unravel everything. Like a weed in a garden, it will choke growth. Back yourself and believe it's possible, because if you don't, the universe won't either.

### 5. Action: Take consistent steps to turn vision into reality

Without execution, nothing happens. Success requires consistent, intentional action. Taking small, daily steps will turn your ideas into achievements. The key is to keep moving, adjust as needed and never stop progressing. Each action builds momentum, compounding over time to create real, measurable progress. Every step forward brings you closer to your ultimate goal.

## Harness self-discipline

Based on what you've just read, you might mistake me for some toga-wearing, tofu-eating, new-age hippie who believes success comes from simply thinking it, saying it and waiting for the universe to deliver it. Nothing could be further from the truth. I'm a hard-nosed lawyer who's battled it out, metaphorically speaking of course, with some of the sharpest operators in the courtroom and the savviest operators in the cutthroat world of Queensland property development. I've gone toe-to-toe with the best (and sometimes the worst) in this country and beyond and I don't deal in mealy-mouthed aphorisms of 'just believe and you'll achieve'. You need to *do*!

To know and to not do is to not know. So, please don't mistake me for someone who believes success just 'manifests' itself. Step 5 is the key. *Action*. You must *do* something. And that takes discipline — the one thing that separates the greats from the gunnas. Granted, not everyone has the natural drive to be disciplined, but here's the secret: you don't have to be born with discipline. You can train your mind to develop it. Here's how.

Imagine for a moment you and your family lived in a bubble 10 metres under water and that once a day, every day, you had to spend 20 minutes going down to the engine room to pump oxygen into that bubble so that you could survive another 24 hours. Would you ever *not* take those 20 minutes to pump oxygen into your bubble? Of course you wouldn't. It would be a death sentence. You'd set every manner of alarms, bells and whistles to ensure that you never, ever missed that 20-minute window to replenish the oxygen in your bubble.

That's the seriousness with which you must practise the disciplines you are about to learn. Spend 20 minutes a day for 30 days and you will see the results. If it doesn't work in the first 30 days, do it for another 30 and then another 30. In a short space of time you'll find that the disciplines come naturally and without thinking or effort, like the Olympian swimmer who naturally wakes at 4 am each morning to go for a swim no matter the conditions. After a while, they don't question it or fight it—they just do it.

This practice will condition your mind in such a way that it will transform your whole thought process, which will in turn, transform your energies so that you will continue to attract good things into your life, with minimal effort. The secret? Consistency. You must do the exercises daily. If you don't, it won't work. It's as simple as that. Without discipline, nothing happens.

### The hidden path to greatness

The renowned opera singer Luciano Pavarotti claimed that if he didn't practise for one day, he would recognise the difference in the tonality and expression of his voice. If he didn't practise for two days in a row, his wife would notice it and if he didn't practise for three days in a row, his audience would notice it. That's how important it is to follow this regime daily.

People look at great athletes, artists and actors and say, 'Oh wow, look how talented and brilliant they are', but what they often don't see is the level of effort required to be brilliant. They just see the results of that effort: the Olympic medal being awarded to the best athlete, the Oscar going to the best actress, the Booker Prize to the best author. I can assure you, those people are ordinary citizens like you and me, with fears and phobias, insecurities and inadequacies.

Are they unique or different? Sometimes, yes, they are built for greatness. An athlete may have fast-twitch fibres that make them inherently suited to sprinting. A singer may have a particular facial structure that gives their voice inordinate resonance. But, in general, most of the brilliant and famous are just simple, ordinary people like you and me who put the work in. And even those who have an innate talent—like the swimmer with big feet or the actor with a photographic memory—still work at making the most of their natural talent. It is the discipline that gives them the edge.

We all have limiting beliefs about what we think we are capable of. But if you learn how to manage those beliefs, reframe them and use them as stepping stones, they become powerful tools for growth. They'll help you uncover who you truly are and what you are meant to do in this life. The moment you break free from these limitations, you'll begin to attract extraordinary opportunities into your life.

## *Harness emotional alignment*

I believe in the power of the mind to shape reality, but not in the way most people think. *The Secret*, by Rhonda Byrne, the wildly bestselling book from the 1990s (that many believed was based on the teachings of Esther and Jerry Hicks, who originally coined the term 'law of attraction') was very impactful for me at the time. The only trouble was it led you to believe that if you sat in a chair and visualised a Ferrari, one would magically appear in your driveway. That's not how it works. I've never been one for wishful thinking. I believe in something more powerful: thoughts backed by action.

I learned early on that my mind was my greatest asset. I knew I wasn't the strongest, the smartest or the most confident kid, but I had an insatiable curiosity about success and I studied it like a scientist. Why did some people have it while others struggled? I realised that successful people weren't just lucky—they operated on a different frequency. They thought differently, spoke differently, made decisions differently. If I wanted success, I needed to think and act like someone who already had it.

But here's the real secret: your energy has to match your goals. If you're stuck in a state of doubt, frustration or negativity, you'll keep attracting situations that reinforce those emotions. You can't expect to build a thriving business, attract the right people or create wealth if your internal state is full of scarcity and fear. You need to be in sync with the outcome you want.

And that's where the chakras come in. The what? The chakras. Chakras are the body's internal energy hubs: seven power centres that align your spirit, mind and body to keep you grounded, focused, creative and connected (see figure 1). When they are all in balance, you experience clarity, flow, confidence and purpose, allowing you to move through life with ease, resilience and alignment to your highest potential. I meditate on them every single day, without fail.

### *Aligning the energy within: my daily chakra practice*

I have always been interested in energy: how it moves, how it flows and most importantly, how to manage and direct it. The ancient concept of the chakras offers a powerful framework for understanding the energy systems within your body. I work with this system every day during meditation to maintain alignment, flow and clarity. When the chakras are open and energy is circulating freely, I am in sync: balanced, grounded and fully alive.

I believe energy flows from our higher self—the spiritual source above the Crown Chakra—and travels downward through each energy centre until it reaches the Root Chakra, anchoring us to the earth. This downward current connects the divine to the physical, the universal to the individual, empowering us to bring our ideas into form through our human experience. Here's how I align each chakra with specific principles that drive both my business and personal life:

- *Root Chakra—grounded in values*

    This is your energetic foundation. It governs security, stability and survival. When grounded in earth's abundance and its gravitational force, you gain the power to manifest your best future. This chakra reminds us that nothing grows without roots and that our values are our anchor.

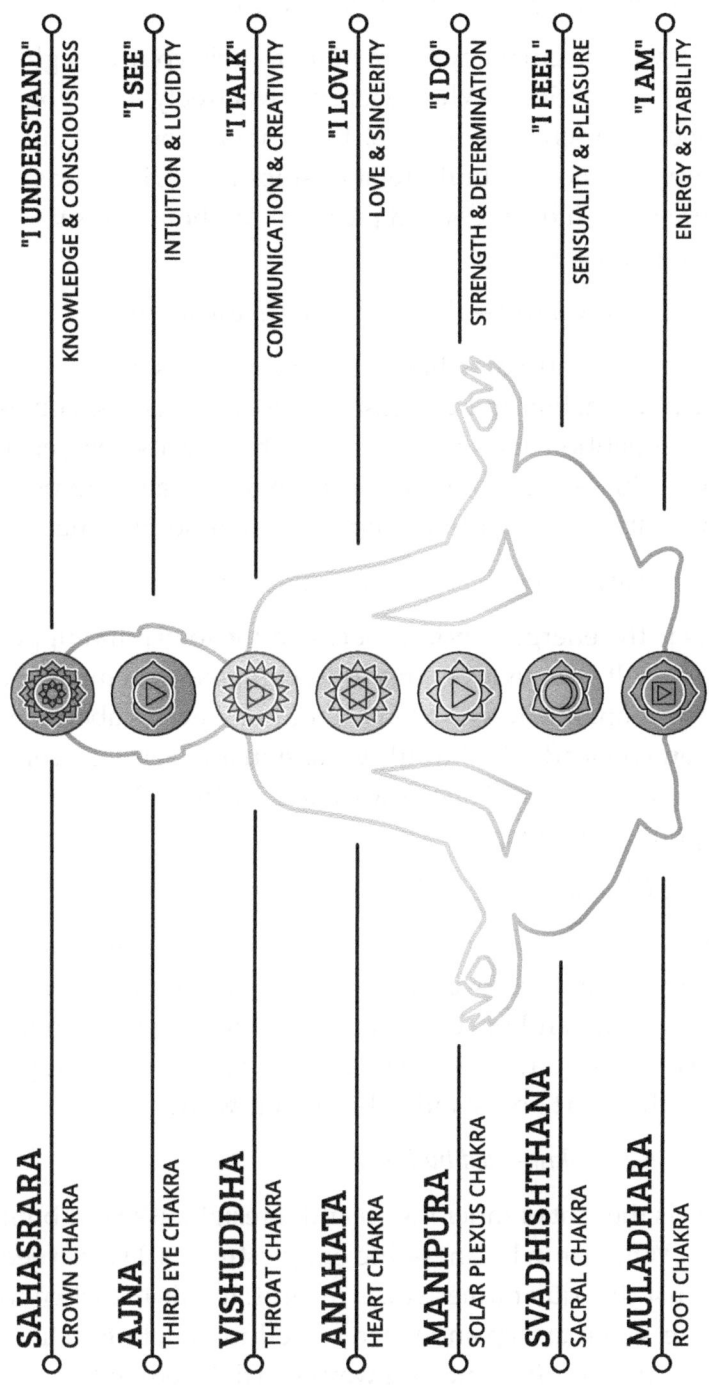

**SAHASRARA**
CROWN CHAKRA

**"I UNDERSTAND"**
KNOWLEDGE & CONSCIOUSNESS

**AJNA**
THIRD EYE CHAKRA

**"I SEE"**
INTUITION & LUCIDITY

**VISHUDDHA**
THROAT CHAKRA

**"I TALK"**
COMMUNICATION & CREATIVITY

**ANAHATA**
HEART CHAKRA

**"I LOVE"**
LOVE & SINCERITY

**MANIPURA**
SOLAR PLEXUS CHAKRA

**"I DO"**
STRENGTH & DETERMINATION

**SVADHISHTHANA**
SACRAL CHAKRA

**"I FEEL"**
SENSUALITY & PLEASURE

**MULADHARA**
ROOT CHAKRA

**"I AM"**
ENERGY & STABILITY

Figure 1: the seven chakras

- *Sacral Chakra—fuelled by creative energy*

  Energy is the currency of creation. It fuels your thoughts, words and actions. When energy flows freely here, you unlock your creative powers. This chakra governs your ability to innovate, build relationships and bring ideas to life in both business and pleasure. Without energy, nothing moves.

- *Solar Plexus Chakra—driven by discipline and process*

  This is the centre of willpower and action. It's where discipline, habits and processes are forged. Success comes from repetition and focus because where focus goes, energy flows. This is the chakra of consistency, courage and personal power. It's the motor that keeps the machine running.

- *Heart Chakra—guided by passion and purpose*

  This is the energetic bridge between the lower and upper chakras. It's about love, gratitude, compassion, empathy and connection. Business isn't just about money, it's about people. When you lead with humility, passion and service, work becomes purpose. Time flows, energy lifts and the universe responds with magic.

- *Throat Chakra—powered by expression*

  This is where your authentic voice lives. For years, I was an observer. But I discovered that my voice, when spoken with clarity, truth and purpose, was one of my greatest strengths. You don't need to shout to be heard; you just need to speak from the heart and stand behind your words.

- *Third-eye Chakra—led by intuition*

  This is the seat of inner vision and foresight. It's your built-in GPS. Whether in business, life or investments, I've learned to trust that quiet inner voice: my gut. It tells me when to pause, when to leap and when something's not right. Intuition often speaks softly, but it's always worth listening to.

- *Crown Chakra—aligned with wisdom*

  This is your connection to universal consciousness. Call it God, Source, the Higher Self or whatever word works for you. It's where wisdom flows. But knowledge alone isn't enough. True wisdom comes from applying what you know through imprinting (remembering), understanding, knowing and doing. Only then can you make sound decisions and live in alignment with your highest self.

When these energy centres are aligned and flowing, life becomes a dance: effortless, joyful and filled with purpose. This practice isn't esoteric to me—it's practical, daily and foundational to my success. When energy moves, life moves. And when you manage your energy, you master your life.

Think of it like tuning a radio. If you want to listen to jazz, you don't tune the radio to 3AW or 2UE and hope they'll play Louis Armstrong or Duke Ellington. You tune in to the station that you know plays jazz 24/7. Life works the same way. You have to align your thoughts, emotions and actions with the frequency of success. When your chakras are balanced and your energy is focused, opportunities start to appear. The right people cross your path. Doors open.

Some call it the law of attraction. I call it working smarter, not harder. You align your chakras, thoughts and actions with the outcome you want and the universe responds. It's not magic—it's physics. And it works.

## *Harness your perspective on life*

As I look back over the decades, I see my life not as one long sprint, but as a series of frames: distinct stages of growth, each with its own purpose. I didn't learn this in a textbook or at a seminar; I discovered it through experience, reflection and a few hard knocks along the way.

Perspective is power. It helps you understand where you are, why you're there and where you're headed next. This principle is about recognising those stages early so you can lead with intention. You don't need to wait until you're 80 to get this clarity. I'm sharing it now, so you can use it today to shape a life that aligns with who you are and what you're becoming. Each frame carries its own set of expectations, challenges and rewards, and each shaped the way I approached life, business and personal fulfillment.

Why is it important to view life in frames? Because it forces you to be intentional. Too many people drift through life without a roadmap, reacting instead of planning. When you define your frames, you gain clarity about where you are and where you're headed. It allows you to focus your energy on the right things at the right time, rather than clinging to the past or rushing the future. It helps you prioritise. Knowing that there's a season for everything prevents you from burning out too early or waiting too long to enjoy life.

# The four frames of life

I've discovered that life doesn't unfold in a straight line; it plays out in distinct stages, each with its own focus, expectations and wisdom. I call these the four frames of life. I could only see this by looking back over my 80 years, a gift and privilege not available to all. I can now see the clear shifts between stages, and how each one brought with it a different purpose and understanding. Knowing which frame you're in not only helps you make better decisions, but it gives you permission to grow, evolve and move forward without worrying about what you should be doing or should have done.

## 1. Parental expectations (age: 0–25)

To me, this time frame is about meeting expectations—doing what parents and society deem necessary, like getting an education, finding stability and preparing for the responsibilities of adulthood.

## 2. Community expectations (age: 26–50)

The purpose of this time frame is to build family, business and reputation. For me, this was the period of hustle, where I gave everything to my career and my community.

## 3. Self expectations (age: 51–75)

I found during this time frame I shifted from obligation to myself to enjoying the fruits of my labour, travelling, deepening my relationship with my wife Lynda and living for *me*.

## 4. Worldly expectations (age: 76–100)

This time frame, which I've now entered, is about learning to let go, give and live: letting go of what no longer serves me, giving back through mentorship and philanthropy, and truly *living* in the most profound way.

• • •

The real benefit of this four-frame mindset is freedom. When you accept that each phase of life has its purpose, you give yourself permission to evolve. You don't have to feel guilty about shifting gears—whether it's stepping away from business, focusing on yourself or dedicating time to giving back. You stop fighting change and start embracing it. Because the truth is, success isn't just about what you build—it's about knowing *when* to build, *when* to enjoy and *when* to give something away.

# How to get the most from this book

This book isn't theory. It's my lived experience. What you're about to read are 50 lessons—bite-sized, practical and powerful—pulled straight from the real-life journey I've taken. The wins, the wipeouts, the comebacks and the breakthroughs. Each lesson is designed to show you not just *what* happened, but *how* I made sense of it, learned from it and turned it into fuel for growth.

Each lesson is matched with a corresponding chakra to help you understand where your power is flowing and where it might be blocked. And to help get those energy wheels spinning, you'll find a mini drill at the end of each lesson. These are simple exercises to align your mindset, reset your energy and get you back on track.

Interwoven among the lessons, you'll find 5-step Misso system drills. The 5-step Misso system is a practical, proven framework for turning intention into action: a method to embed what you've learned into your daily life. These short, powerful drills are designed to be done anywhere, anytime. Do them consistently and you'll start to see real results. You don't need to be spiritual, or even fully believe in these lessons or drills. You just need to be curious and committed. Work the system and the system will work for you. If you trust in the process, follow the steps and do the exercises, the results will astound you.

And finally, if you're keen to dive deeper into the ideas explored in this book, I've created an online community at www.think2be .com.au. It's a space where you can access resources, explore online courses and connect with like-minded people who are on the same path. Whether you're just starting out or already well on your way, it's a place to keep learning, growing and building momentum, together.

Let's get started.

# #1

# Work with what you have

I was a sickly child, an acne-ridden teenager and an anxious adolescent. My childhood was not easy. It all started at birth.

It was 14 December 1945, Ceylon, now better known as Sri Lanka. We were known as the 'Burghers' of Ceylon, a small Eurasian ethnic group descended from the Portuguese, the Dutch and other Europeans who settled in Ceylon. The world was still reeling from the aftermath of World War II and my parents were trying to re-build a post-war life in this tropical paradise. Little did they know the battle that awaited them in the delivery room of Kandy General Hospital.

I entered this world feet-first, a breech baby gasping for air. The delivery was complicated. My mother nearly died and I wasn't far behind. 'He probably won't live through the night,' they said.

I defied medical expectations and lived, but I was in an incubator for many weeks, my tiny body fighting for survival. My father later told me how he'd stand for hours, watching my chest rise and fall, praying for each breath to be followed by another.

As I grew, it became clear that my difficult entry into the world was just the beginning. Ceylon's tropical climate, while paradise for some, was a breeding ground of illness for children like me. By the age of five, I had already battled a host of respiratory diseases, which set me up for a lifetime of ill-health. I was particularly prone to severe tonsillitis, which often left me bedridden for days, sometimes weeks. The doctors repeatedly recommended that my tonsils be removed, but my mother, a staunch believer in natural healing, refused. She believed that surgery was unnecessary and that with the right care and prayer, my body could heal itself.

One of the most debilitating conditions I suffered from was migraines. These weren't just headaches; they were full-blown, excruciating assaults that knocked me out for days at a time. The first one hit when I was just 10 years old. I remember the searing pain, the nausea, the unbearable sensitivity to light and sound. My parents tried everything—painkillers, herbal remedies, even acupuncture—but nothing provided lasting relief. These migraines became a constant in my life, a dark cloud that hovered over me, ready to strike at any moment.

And so, I endured the pain, the asthma, the fever, the headaches and the endless cycles of illness and pneumonia, all the while growing stronger in spirit, if not in body.

But despite these challenges, I refused to see myself as weak or incapable. My parents were my pillars of strength. Especially my father. He had his own share of health battles, having suffered from rheumatic fever as a child, but he never let it define him. He would often sit with me and share stories of people who had overcome huge odds to achieve greatness. One of his favourite stories was that of Charles Atlas, a man who, through sheer willpower and determination, transformed himself from a '97-pound weakling' into Mr Universe. Other nights, we'd pray together. These weren't your typical bedtime prayers. They were raw, honest conversations with God (or the universal consciousness—whatever you want to call it) where I'd pour out my fears, my frustrations, my hopes. These rituals and stories became my anchor and taught me the power of faith, strength and mindfulness long before these became modern-day buzzwords. They resonated deeply with me and planted the seeds of resilience and tenacity that would inform my entire existence.

## Lesson #1 takeaway

Strength doesn't come from ideal conditions—it comes from how you respond to imperfect ones. When you stop waiting for the perfect health, perfect timing or perfect start and instead work with what you've got, you build real momentum. Your perceived limitations can become your greatest source of strength if you choose to meet them with courage and belief. It's not about what you lack—it's about what you think and what you do with what you have.

*Chakra:* Root (Muladhara)

*Primary energy focus:* Grounding, resilience and inner stability in times of struggle

### Drill to strengthen the Root Chakra

- Sit with your feet flat on the ground. Close your eyes.
- Take five deep, steady breaths, inhaling through the nose, exhaling through the mouth.
- Place your hands over your lower belly and say, out loud, 'I am safe. I am strong. I have everything I need to begin'.
- Open your eyes and write down three ways your past struggles have made you stronger today.

# #2
# Listen to your inner compass

My father owned a small law practice in Ceylon. In the course of his work, he had the occasion to meet with a senior monk from the local monastery. This monk wasn't just any religious figure; he was a man of great spiritual insight and wisdom, revered by many throughout the land for his ability to see beyond the ordinary. My father asked the monk to prophesise as to what was in store for our family.

The monk foretold that my father would face dramatic changes in his life and that he was destined to live in a foreign country. He also said, 'Watch out for your second son. He is a special child, gifted with a range of powers that will emerge in later years. He has the power to manifest great things beyond the ordinary and will far surpass your achievements'. Considering I was that second son and I was a sickly, skinny and frail boy who could barely get out of bed without collapsing in pain from migraines, this was a revelation to me and my father!

My father never forgot that visit from the monk and that prophecy guided him in the early days of my upbringing. When I was old enough to understand, my father shared that prophecy with me. I took it to heart and it became the guiding light in my life: a beacon of hope that fuelled my desire to overcome the adversity of the ill-health that had become my constant companion.

In September 1956, when I was 10 years old, the monk's prophecy that we would live in a foreign country came true. Political turmoil and violence had erupted in Ceylon, forcing us to abandon our homeland and seek safety elsewhere. Within three weeks of the surge in fighting that filled our streets, my father had packed up our entire belongings into a few suitcases, withdrawn from his law firm (which still operates in Kandy today), withdrawn us from school, grabbed as much cash as he could and left. Everything else we owned was surrendered to the government of the day.

It was a massive shift and a severe disruption to the sweet life we had been living, but it proved to be one of the best decisions my father ever made for our family's wellbeing. Had he stayed, we would have all risked being arrested, beaten or possibly killed.

We migrated to Australia and settled in Redcliffe, a small, coastal town 40 kilometres north of Brisbane, a world away from the grand life of the British colony we had known in Ceylon. Everything was different: the language, the climate and especially the culture. Discrimination was everywhere. The White Australia Policy was still casting a long shadow and anyone who didn't fit the Anglo ideal felt it. Even someone like me, with light-brown skin and a European name, was treated as an outsider. Religious discrimination was at play too. Catholics were pitched against Protestants and both experienced bigotry for being on the wrong side. Back in Ceylon, we had had servants, and to move from a life of having things done for us to having no domestic help was a huge transition for my parents and us. In short, the shift to Australia was challenging for our entire family.

I attended primary school in the Brisbane suburb of Humpybong before moving on to De La Salle College, a Catholic high school in Redcliffe. I was of the Presbyterian faith and had attended a Church of England school back in Ceylon, so to be thrust into this unfamiliar Catholic world of strange ritualistic smells and bells was deeply unsettling. As time went on, however, the teachings at De La Salle began to strengthen my own beliefs and reinforced the importance of maintaining a strong connection to my Christian faith.

I had a hard time at school. I was a skinny, scrawny kid with acne and bat-ears, was constantly sick and had terrible headaches. I struggled through every grade, yet despite this, the school thought I was too bright for my Grade 6 class, so they promoted me up a year. I was already having a hard time and this 'upgrade' just made it worse. From then on, I really fell behind in every way—academically, athletically, socially, mentally—and this struggle continued right through to Year 12.

To distract me from the nightmare that school had become, I took on a huge array of part-time jobs to make money, which ignited my passion for entrepreneurship and commerce, but school remained a torment from start to finish. In those tough early years, I found solace in my Christian faith. My grounding in Christianity came from my formative time at the world-renowned Trinity College in Kandy, Ceylon, a place I remember with deep fondness.

From a young age, I felt very much that I was 'hardwired to God' in that I was always aware of the universal source of energy that connected us all and that there was a divine presence that underpinned the essence of every sentient being on the planet. This faith in a cosmic connection, as well as the foundational truths, buoyed me through those difficult teenage years and provided me with the strength to deal with my early adversities.

## Lesson #2 takeaway

Your inner compass knows the way, even when the world feels unfamiliar or uncertain. When you listen deeply to the quiet knowing within, you'll find the strength to act with clarity, even in chaos. Intuition, faith and vision aren't abstract ideas, they're

*(continued)*

practical tools for navigating upheaval and transformation. Life may push you off course, but your inner guidance will always bring you back. Trust it, even when no-one else does.

*Chakra:* Third-eye (Ajna)

*Primary energy focus:* Inner vision, intuition and spiritual insight

### Drill to strengthen the Third-eye Chakra

- Sit quietly with your eyes closed.
- Take three deep breaths and place two fingers gently between your eyebrows.
- Ask yourself, 'What do I already know, but haven't acknowledged?'
- Listen for the first word, image or feeling that arises.
- Whisper this affirmation: 'I trust what I see within'.

# #3

# Embrace adversity

The most significant event of my childhood occurred when I was 12 years old, one year after arriving in Australia. It was a seemingly insignificant incident, but I can see now that it changed the course of my life. Being Sri Lankan, I loved cricket. How could I not? It was our national sport. To me, it was more than just a game; it was a passion, a memory of home, a way to connect with other boys in my new school and to feel a part of something.

But a lunchtime game of cricket changed everything. I was positioned at silly mid-off, one of the most dangerous fielding positions because you have to stand just metres from the batter and directly behind them. When the ball comes at you, there's very little time to react or get out of the way (which is why the position is called 'silly'—because no-one should be standing that close!). Of course, you can guess what happened next. Yes, I was hit in the head with a cricket ball at full speed. In the left eye, to be specific. I dropped to the ground, blinded by the blood that was oozing out of my eye. I was no stranger to pain—the migraines had inured me to that—but this pain was so intense I nearly passed out, right there on the cricket pitch. The teachers called an ambulance and I was rushed to hospital, terrified I might lose the vision in my eye. As if being bandy-legged and bat-eared wasn't enough, it looked like I might now end up blind too!

The doctor stitched up my eye and the physical scars on my face healed, but the emotional scars ran far deeper. The incident irrevocably changed something within me. Up until then, I had been a sickly boy, but I had been a happy and lively one, full of beans and keen to extract as much fun and passion from life as I could. Despite my shyness, I was always eager to participate in sports and to hang out with the other kids, doing what kids did. I wanted to be just like the other boys who were bigger, stronger and more confident.

But after the incident, everything changed. I stopped playing cricket, I stopped playing with my friends, I stopped playing everything. I withdrew from all social contact and started to watch life from the sidelines. It was as if a light inside of me had been switched off. I shied away from any physical encounter or interaction, convinced that something similar might happen again. I now lived with fear all the time. This withdrawal from school activities, contact sports and then withdrawal from life itself did not go unnoticed. And when the schoolboys sensed my fear, they left no stone unturned in exploiting it. The teasing was relentless, which made me feel even more isolated, inadequate and alone. This lack of self-esteem fed into my studies too. School was already difficult, but now it was impossible. I had struggled with going up a grade and this bullying made me even more distracted and demotivated. It took me years to overcome the emotional impact of that cricket incident. I think I am still getting over it.

However, what the incident did do was force me to look inwards and develop other aspects of myself that didn't rely on physical strength or athletic ability. I turned to books, music and most importantly, to my faith. The cricket incident may have shattered my confidence in schoolwork and friendships, but it pushed me to cultivate a different kind of strength—a mental, emotional and spiritual resilience—that would serve me well in years to come.

While my peers seemed to enjoy relatively carefree childhoods, I constantly faced doubts, difficulties and hardships, as well as all the other limitations imposed by my frail physical build. However, this 'blessing' contained the seeds of my greatest strengths. With few outer resources, I had no choice but to dive inwards and develop an inner life rich with imagination, vision and an iron will. I had always loved Walt Disney cartoons and immersed myself even further into that universe of make-believe worlds where everything was possible. I went deeper into my imagination and found an inner determination to turn those make-believe realms into reality. In short, I cultivated an unshakeable belief that I could conjure magic through focused thought alone. My imagination became a muscle I worked on and I used it to vividly envision the successful self-made man I knew I could become. With nothing to lose, I went all-in on developing my powers of creative visualisation and affirmation.

## Lesson #3 takeaway

Adversity is not an obstacle — it's a training ground. Every setback, every painful experience and every challenge you face is an opportunity to develop inner strength, resilience and vision. You may not control what happens to you, but you always control how you respond. The moments that shake you the most often hold the seeds of your greatest strengths, if you have the courage to look within and transform them into power.

*Chakra:* Solar Plexus (Manipura)

*Primary energy focus:* Personal power, resilience and self-worth

### Drill to strengthen the Solar Plexus Chakra

- Sit upright. Place your hands just above your navel.
- Close your eyes and breathe into this centre.
- Say out loud, or in your mind, 'I am strong. I am unstoppable. I trust in my inner power'.
- Visualise a golden flame glowing brighter with each breath, burning away doubt and fuelling confidence.